To

Leah —

Because I

want you to know —

John

6/30/19

John N. DeFoore

The FOOT SOLDIER

outskirts
press

Outskirts Press, Inc.
http://www.outskirtspress.com

ISBN: 978-1-4787-3373-7

Outskirts Press and the "OP" logo are trademarks belonging to Outskirts Press, Inc.

PRINTED IN THE UNITED STATES OF AMERICA

This is the way I remember the events.

Seventy years have passed and some of the memories, thank God, are dim. Some are gone.

Some will never leave.

I will not tell this story completely. I never could.

This story will contain a few facts. It is not the whole story. Mostly it is details. The details are burned into my brain with a red-hot banding iron.

I live with them today as if the events occurred last night.

CONTENTS

YOU NEED TO KNOW THIS

There are a lot of levels in war. They reach all the way from the President of the United State to the foot soldier who digs a hole and sleeps in the ground every night.

I was in the Infantry. The infantry is the individual on the ground that does the killing. He may or may not have food. He may or may not have medical treatment. He may or may not get mail. This is war at its dirtiest and lowest levels of combat.

The foot soldier is the one who engages in hand-to-hand combat with the enemy. He is the one who goes down the ramp when the landing barge hits shore. He is the one who picks up a rifle and goes through the jungle on patrol.

For this man, war is blood, mud and guts.

The war for the Infantryman is different from anything else in the world.

THE WAR

Someone has suggested that I write this book just about the war and the memories I have.

Strange that now I am trying to remember what I have spent 70 years trying to forget.

This book is for my four sons, because they have been so patient and loving with their father.

And to my wife whom I love---Marion Sue---who has understood when no understanding was possible.

THIS IS IMPORTANT---THE YEARS HAVE COLORED AND CHANGED MY MEMORIES. I DO NOT CLAIM TO HAVE ALL THE DETAILS CORRECT. THIS IS THE WAY IT COMES TO MY MIND TODAY. SOME THINGS I WISH I COULD REMEMBER---OTHERS I HAVE TRIED UNSUCCESSFULLY TO FORGET. SO PLEASE KEEP THAT IN MIND WHEN YOU READ THIS.

For those who need to know:

I am:

Major John N. DeFoore

Serial no. 0414908

2nd Bn. 155 Infantry

31st Division

(New Guinea, Morotai, Mindinao Philippines)

Aftermath of Bombing

19 YEARS OLD AND IN FEDERAL SERVICE

(1939) 19 years old---I was back in college. (Had dropped out a year earlier and was working on a highway crew driving a bulldozer. My best friends suicide sent me back to college---scared to death).

I was living in the dormitory after a year, working in a dairy milking 20 cows, twice a day, by hand.

I had been awarded a fellowship in the Biology Department, so I left the dairy and moved on campus. I felt so very fortunate. For extra money, I worked with the campus handyman nicknamed "Doctor Luke". We had the job of keeping all the toilets on campus functioning. I helped.

The matron of one of the dorms let me sleep in the basement of the dorm and I did not have to pay the dorm fee---in a room partially filled with bags of cement. Later I moved upstairs and had a real room.

One of my friends said to me one day, "Don't you play a musical instrument? The band here is a National Guard Band and they pay one dollar for every rehearsal." I immediately signed up. Every dollar helped.

Strange---several months later the band director made the announcement: "I am sorry to announce that we have been mobilized into federal service. We are going to Camp Blanding, Florida, for one year of military training. "

Of course I did not want to go. I knew there was a war in Europe and some guy named Hitler was causing trouble. I really did not know more than that.

I went to the band director and told him that I was sorry I would not be able to go. I had other plans and wanted to finish my college education, etc., etc.,etc.

He smiled and said, "Son, when you joined this band you joined the National Guard. When you joined the National Guard you joined the Army. You have no choice. You are going with us."

But then I was told that I would receive $18.00 a month with all expenses paid, so I went---What else could I do?

One cold December morning I went to a room and turned in my civilian clothes and got my army uniform. I did not dream of the things that would happen in my life. Shortly after I boarded a train for Florida and "my year of military training"---which turned out to be six years.

MY COMMISSION AS A SECOND LIEUTENANT

I had previously had some training during the summers at what was called the Citizens Military Training Camp. The camp was in Louisiana and paid thirty dollars for one months training. I had attended four summers of the training camps.

This information was on my service record when I signed in for the band. Later, I had an inquiry from Division Headquarters and was asked to submit a request for a commission. (This was early in the war and there was a demand for officers). Later, I went with a group of men to take competitive examinations to see who would get commissions.

Several months later I got an order to report to Division Headquarters. I had no idea what the problem was but I went.

I was ushered into the office of General John C. Persons, Commander of the 31st Infantry Division and he said, "Private DeFoore, you are being promoted to Second Lieutenant". I was totally shocked and could hardly believe what I was hearing.

Then he said, "Do you have a shirt with epaulets?"

I said, "No Sir." He said, "Go to the PX and buy one." I said, "Sir, I have no money. Can you lend me $2.00?" He smiled and handed me two dollars. I later paid him back.

(In a strange way, the general and I sort of became friends. On two occasions he called me and asked me to escort his daughter to a division dance. She was drop dead beautiful and a great dancer, so this was not a problem at all. Later he asked me to be his Aide de Camp and I refused---not a smart decision.)

I went back to the band area where I lived and walked into the orderly room. Everyone saluted me and it felt great.

(Earlier a friend and I had started a business of starching shirts and blocking hats. We charged 25 cents for the shirts and $1.50 to block the hats. When I came back to the area as a second lieutenant my friend said, "I know you are an officer, but you still have to help me wash these shirts." I did.)

I moved from the band area to "Officers Row". I had a tent of my own and an orderly to polish my shoes and brass and wash my clothes. I was on top of the world. I left the band and was assigned to a rifle company as a platoon commander.

PEARL HARBOR

Air Raid

One Sunday afternoon I was listening to the broadcast of a symphony concert and the program was interrupted with an announcement: "We are sorry to announce that the Japanese air force has bombed Pearl Harbor."

My world changed.

Our division was alerted. We left camp that night and went to the overseas highway that connected mainland Florida to Key West. There were 27 bridges on the highway. There was a very important submarine base at Key West and the highway had to be kept open.

America was at war. When we took over the bridges we found that German saboteurs had put boxes of dynamite under the bridges and had planned to blow up all the bridges to Key West. We removed the dynamite.

There was no longer any thought of coming home.

President Roosevelt declared war on Japan and then later Germany. For several months we had the task of securing the bridges on the overseas highway.

I learned that a new division of the army was being organized called the Paratroopers. After some inquiry I learned that the pay was twice what I was making, plus there was a $25.00 bonus every time you jumped out of the plane. I could hardly wait for a transfer.

I got a two weeks leave to go to Fort Benning, Georgia, to sign-up for the paratroopers. I visited my home in Mississippi on the way to Georgia. My mother asked why I was going to Fort Benning and I explained what my plans were---

She said: "You are not going to join that bunch. I am not going to have you jumping out of an airplane. You go right back to your outfit."

What could I say? Obediently, like a child, I went back to my outfit---this probably saved my life.

ENCOUNTER WITH GENERAL PATTON

Combat Crew

I had transferred from the rifle company and had been assigned as commander of the Anti-tank company. We had trained for several months and then we went to Louisiana for training.

The exercise started and we were at war. I deployed my guns. I built a road block on the highway. I had the umpires ready to score my work. I knew a column of tanks was coming down this road.

I soon heard the sound of the motors and saw 15 tanks in line. We hit the four lead tanks with flour bags (to indicate they had been destroyed) and the umpire called them "out of action". The road was blocked with logs.

Immediately, the turret popped open on the lead tank; a man stood up and screamed; "Who in the hell is in charge of this Company?"

I saluted. Then very proudly, I responded with my name and rank and said:

"I claim four of your tanks destroyed. Four of your tanks are out of action and this road block stops your column."

This individual (whom I later learned was Lt. Col. George C. Patton---later to be the famous General Patton who ran wild into Russia) shook his fist at me and said: "Lieutenant get those +*&^% logs out of the road and clean that flour off my tanks or I am going to run over you and every _*&^%$ man in your company."

I did exactly what he told me to do.

What else could I do?

(If I had known the kind of man he was at that moment I would have joined his outfit and followed him all through the war. He was one tuff soldier.)

OCEAN VOYAGE

We were shipped to Camp Pickett, Va. and we knew it was the Port of Embarkation---slang term POE.

We were marched into huge buildings—took off all our clothing just inside the front door---examined by several doctors as we were shuttled across the room---given several shots in both arms at the same time---and given new clothes and duffle bags as we were ushered out the door on the opposite side of the building.

We then were sent back to our barracks---told we could not communicate with anyone---and at midnight in total blackout we were marched down to the pier and loaded onto a ship. I think the name of the ship was Maniora or something like that---of course the guys quickly named it the Manure. The ship was a cargo vessel that had been modified to carry troops.

The bunk beds below deck were five bunks high. There was some air conditioning but it was very hot below. I asked for, and got, Officer of the Deck duty so I could spend time on deck. I made friends with the captain of the ship. He knew the stars in detail and knew the planets. At night, of course, we sailed in total blackout conditions, we would sit on deck and he would talk about the stars for hours. I did not think much about war---just stayed in the present and enjoyed the ocean voyage.

But thoughts of the war kept coming into my thoughts. The captain asked me if I was ready to kill a human being. I answered in the affirmative though I knew on my insides it was not settled.

Our ship zigzagged all the way across the Pacific.

This maneuver was necessary to avoid the attacks from the submarines. I never did understand the purpose, but I am sure the navy knew more about this than I did.

We were not told our destination until we had passed through the Panama Canal. I really thought we were going to Europe until that time, and then it was announced that our destination was Buna, New Guinea. We were also told that it was not a combat zone at that time.

After about 45 days we pulled into the harbor at Buna. I was glad to be off the ship even if we were in New Guinea.

Letter Home

AGNES

My story would not be complete without including the story of this woman.

She was the wife of the man who served as my first sergeant during most of the war. I had known them in the states. I had visited in their home many times before we went overseas.

She was beautiful. She was a good cook. She had a great personality, but her dominant trait was her love for her husband. I have never seen a woman who loved a man the way Agnes loved Rogers.

Every time there were visitors allowed on the base she was first through the gate. Every time we had leave privileges, Rogers was the first one going home to see Agnes. They were inseparable but they were also loving and kind to others. I had lots of meals in their home. She was a great cook.

One time, our unit was being moved to Louisiana for Maneuvers. We were in a long military convoy escorted by the highway patrol. In the middle of the convoy there was one civilian vehicle---

It was Agnes.

Of course this was against every military procedure. At one point the General, who was leading the column drove down the line of vehicles and saw the civilian car. He walked up to the car, saw Agnes, and screamed: "Woman, what in the hell are you doing in this convoy?"

Agnes answered very quietly, "I am going to Louisiana. My husband is in the convoy."

The General shouted: "Get that car out of the way and keep it off the *&^%$ road. You cannot travel in a military convoy."

Agnes answered, "This is a public highway and I am going to Louisiana just like you are."

The General looked at her, scratched his head, calmed down a bit and then he said, "And what is your name?"

Agnes said, "I will not tell you my name because it might get my husband in trouble."

(This was unheard of. No one would ever speak to a General Officer in this manner.)

The General was completely stunned. He stood there and looked at Agnes, took a deep breath and then he smiled, leaned back and laughed. After a minute or two he said, "Lady, you can go with us anywhere you wish. I am glad to have you in this convoy."

He instructed the Military Police that she could travel with any military convoy anytime she chose. The convoy continued to Louisiana---sixty-two military vehicles and one black civilian car driven by Agnes.

Months later, in another state, we were loading ship to go overseas. The port was dark. It was the tightest of security; the lights were all blacked out and no one was allowed anywhere near the docks where the ships were loading.

I was standing on the deck of the ship watching the loading process and I could see the large fence that bordered the docks. There was one single dim light at the gate and I could barely see the outline of a small female figure standing there---

It was Agnes.

(We went overseas. Years later Rogers was wounded and shipped home. When I returned after the war, I visited them in their home. Sometime later she died and I stood with Rogers by the side of her grave and we both told her goodbye.

I have never known-or seen-or heard of-another Agnes.)

2 Native Boys

NEW GUINEA

We started training immediately. Everything was focused on surviving in the tropical heat and in the jungle. It was a strange and somewhat mysterious world for all of us.

Several days after our arrival I was called to Regimental Headquarters and told that I was being ordered to go and live in a native village for one month. Then at the end of the time I would return and teach the soldiers about surviving in the jungle.

The next day three New Guinea policemen came to my outfit. I accompanied them into the jungle for a three hour walk and then we came to a small village.

I was introduced to a New Guinea soldier named Gogooba. He was very short, but obviously strong, and he had a huge head of bushy hair. I felt comfortable immediately with him. He told me in "pigeon English" that he was a very brave soldier and had killed more than 100 Japs. He also told me that I was not to worry because he was being paid to take care of me. I felt safe with him.

I stayed in the village for one month. I had a bamboo platform for a bed with a banana leaf roof. I had no contact with anyone else in the village. I ate army rations—Australian bully beef and hard tack that I had brought with me. Each day we left the village and went into the jungle.

Gogooba told me what plants I could eat, where to drink water, what snakes were dangerous, how to listen to certain night sounds and many other ways to stay alive in the jungle. He taught me how to move in jungle grass and trees, and at the end of the month I was feeling comfortable in my new world.

Googoba carried a rifle with a bandolier of cartridges over his shoulder. However, his main weapon or tool was a machete, which he used as skillfully as a surgeon uses a scalpel. I was constantly amazed at his skill with that huge knife.

My name, to him, was something that sounded like "Joan" or "Jon". His voice was always quiet and almost a whisper. He never raised his voice at me but one time. That time he saved my life.

There was a witch doctor in the village. Googoba told me that he did not want me in the village because I was bad medicine. I always avoided him and gave him plenty of room so he would not have to meet me. One day however, I was travelling alone from one village to another and I met this witch doctor on a very narrow footpath.

It was narrow and bordered by very tall grass on either side. It was obvious that one of us had to step aside. We stood still and faced each other. He screamed at me. I screamed back. He waved his arms and lunged at me. I waved my arms and lunged at him. He spit on me. I spit back at him.

Finally, I thought this could go on forever and so I stepped aside in the tall grass and he strutted by me and kept looking back and leering at me as he moved down the trail. I told Googoba about the encounter and he said, "Never-never do this. He make you dead."

This month of training probably saved my life. I later spent three weeks lost in the jungle in Mindanao in the Philippines and barely survived.

It was hard to leave Gogooba, but I was ready to get back to my outfit. He told me as I was leaving that if I needed him he would always come to me.

Lt. Burt

MY FIRST FIRE FIGHT

Late one afternoon we were called to headquarters and the Colonel said he was sending a battalion reinforced approximately 10 miles up the beach to capture a Japanese airstrip.

My company was not assigned to go. I asked to go as an observer. I had never been under fire and I wanted to get my "baptism of fire" when I was not commanding troops. I did not know how I would perform in combat and I felt it was time for me to find out.

I was attached to the headquarters unit. The next morning we left before daylight and moved up the beach and through the jungle. We arrived at the airstrip at 2 pm.

There was no opposition. We moved in and occupied the airstrip with a minimum of resistance.

WHAT WE DID NOT KNOW---was that these were seasoned Japanese troops. They knew we were coming. They allowed us to come into the area and then they moved in behind us so that we could not go back the way we had come. They had closed off our way of escape.

All of a sudden, all hell broke loose. We were being fired on from every direction. There were snipers in all of the trees and some were dug in holes and covered over with brush. It was bedlam and our troops were panicked. We were under attack from every direction.

A machine gun opened up in front of me and I hit the ground and hugged the dirt. I could feel the wind of the bullets flying over my back.

I panicked. I could not breathe. My blood turned to ice water. I was paralyzed---until---I heard a voice. It was a chaplain lying in the grass next to me. Through the grass he handed me a box of vanilla wafers and said; "Hey man, have a vanilla wafer. My mothers sends these to me and they are the best you will ever eat."

I breathed. My blood turned warm. I could think. I took the box and ate a couple of vanilla wafers and they were delicious. I handed the box back to the chaplain.

I started to think. My brain cleared. (I had the specific thought: I will not let any man be braver than I am.) So I got busy. We neutralized the machine gun with a volley of grenades. I got a group of guys together and we fought our way through the Jap lines and made our way back home. We travelled through the jungle and got back to our safe area around midnight. We even brought one man home on a make-shift stretcher (a pancho over two rifles with bayonets attached.)

Strange to say, I never felt fear in combat after that experience.

(Some time later I heard the chaplain had been killed trying to rescue a wounded man at night. When they recovered his body the next day they found a vanilla wafer box inside his jacket. It was empty.)

FYI---when you come to my office you can look in the bottom right hand drawer of my desk and you will find some vanilla wafers. I always keep some there. Help yourself.

Lt. Wallace (Rest Camp)

MOUNTAIN TOP

Sunday afternoons were usually free. For the first month we were on New Guinea we were training for combat and being issued supplies and getting supplies.

After worship services I would roam through the jungle in the surrounding areas. I finally climbed a small mountain and found a beautiful view that overlooked the entire area of the harbor. It was filled with ships and tugs. They were busy, of course, frantically trying to get our unit ready for combat.

Occasionally I would see a large ship moving out of the harbor. I knew it was going back to the States.

I have difficulty describing the feelings I had when I watched those ships sailing out of the harbor.

I imagined myself on board. I pictured myself in a stateroom, on board the ship, drinking coffee and smiling. I consciously tried to transport myself-without success-from the mountain top to the ship. It did not work. I stayed on the mountain top. (In my mind's eye---after all the years---I can still see those ships leaving the harbor bound for home.)

I did this several weekends until we moved deeper into the jungle. It was a regular Sunday event and I enjoyed the fantasy.

The reality however proved to be stronger than the fantasy.

I thought about my three brothers and wondered where they were. My older brother was in the Marines and he had fought at Guadacanal. The brother just younger than I, Charles, was in the Sea Bees and I think he was on Formosa. My youngest brother, Jud, was in a submarine somewhere in the Mediterranean.

I wondered and wondered and wondered. How long would the war last? Would I survive? Would I be brave? Could I lead my men into battle? Was my faith in God strong enough to let me be the leader and man that I should be? Were my Mother and my sister OK at home? Did she have enough food to eat? Were my three brothers still alive? Were they wounded?

The mountain answered not a word.

So I walked slowly back to my tent-the real world-and into reality.

THE FIRST TIME I KILLED A HUMAN BEING

I trained a lot of men. At one time I had charge of a training bat-talion---1800 new recruits. I took great pride in my responsibility to train these men so they would be ready for combat. When the 6 weeks period was over they were ready.

I taught them to kill. I taught them to hate. I taught them to survive. They were really combat ready when I finished my work. I took great pride in training new recruits to be soldiers.

Strange to say, I had never really settled it for myself. My nag-ging question stayed with me:

"Am I really going to kill another human being?"

One year later, after 3 months in the jungle I went on patrol with 11 other guys. We were sent out to find a group of Japanese that been making trouble for us for a few days.

We had travelled several hours through the jungle and we came onto a large field covered with what we called "kunai grass". It grew about 10 feet tall and was very thick.

I had stopped at the edge of the field and laid down to rest. Suddenly I saw the grass moving about 10 feet away. Then I saw a Jap lie down and start looking all around him.

My first thought was—kill him. Then I paused for just a second and said, "Is this what I really want to do?" Instantly I saw him turn and knew he had seen me. He started to turn his rifle toward me and I shot him 6 times (I had a Thompson sub-machine gun). I waited for a minute, then I saw him move and I shot him three more times.

I waited to see if he had friends to come out and then I went to him and searched his body. I found a few papers and kept them to send to the rear.

That was the only enemy contact we had that day. When I got back to the rear and crawled into my foxhole for the night, I said to myself: "So you are a murderer. You have killed a man."

I did not feel guilt. I gave it no more thought. I completely dismissed it from my mind. I bowed my head and went to sleep. I killed many more Japs after that and never gave it a thought.

⸻))•((⸻

(Since the war I have had lots of questions. I do not know that I have ever reconciled the question in my mind. I do want to say, however, that I have not killed one single person since I got back to the States!)

P.S. In reading numerous books on philosophy and related subjects I ran across a quote, "There is no difference between homicide and suicide." (Source unknown)

Native Village

AMPHIBIOUS LANDING ON MOROTAI ISLAND

We got our orders in a tent near a beach in New Guinea. It was night-no lights. We assembled in the tent of the Regimental Commander, Colonel Hanna.

Assignments were made. First wave would be a rifle company, second wave another rifle company, and my company (the Cannon Company) would go in on the third wave.

We got information about the defense of the beach, the number-approximate-of enemy defenders, and other important facts. The initial report was that there was no coral and that the landing barges should make it all the way to shore.

The actual time of the landing would be announced later. The estimate was that we would have 30% casualties. Then, an ominous note when the Colonel said, "The wounded will be loaded on landing barges when possible. The dead and dying will be left on the beach."

It was specifically stated there were no coral problems that would prevent the barges from reaching the shore.

After loading on the ships---we were underway two days and then anchored offshore to watch the bombing and strafing.

It was a great show. All the naval firepower was directed to the beach in addition to the Air Force bombing and strafing. This made a powerful statement about our strength.

The next morning, in the dark, the first two waves were loaded into the landing craft and circled until it was their time to hit the beach.

My unit had been loaded on a LST (larger ship—landing ship tank). We arrived at our point of departure; were loaded on landing barges and headed for the shore.

About 50 yards from the shore we heard an awful scraping sound that told us our barge was hitting coral. (In the intelligence briefing the weight of the barges loaded with men determined the draft of the landing barge. My barges were much heavier because of the weight of our equipment and therefore rode lower in the water and we were stuck on solid coral rock.)

I looked at the naval guy running the barge and he shouted, "Unload". There was nothing I could do. He dropped the ramp and we drove the trucks, guns and bulldozer off into the water.

(In an amphibious landing the barges are never supposed to be still. When they are still they make great targets for enemy fire. So unloading had to be done as quickly as possible to keep from losing the landing barges.)

Our vehicles and guns were dumped into what I guess was 10-12 feet of water. All my men made it ashore except 4 or 5 that we lost to snipers.

All of my equipment was underwater. I knew we were in serious trouble.

Finally, my motor sergeant, whose name was Pixley came to me and said, "What are you going to do, Long John." I still remember his question and the way he looked at me and smiled.

I answered immediately, "We are going to find a truck with a winch; commandeer it and haul out our equipment."

We found a truck; forced the driver out over his protest; drove it to the beach; dug in the trucks two front wheels in the sand; stripped down to our underwear and started out to our vehicles.

When we started wading out Pixley looked at me and said, "Can you swim?" We both laughed.

We located the bulldozer first. Thankful it was not as heavy in the water as it was on land. We hitched the cable and swam back to the shore.

Inch by inch we brought the bulldozer to the beach.

(The snipers were still busy on the beach. As well as I can remember they did not bother us at this point.)

After we got the bulldozer ashore we brought in two guns (105 mm howitzers) and I started a crew draining the recoil mechanism and putting in fresh oil.

We worked all day. I had a crew draining oil and gas from guns and vehicles while Pixley and I brought them to the beach. We tired quickly and had some other guys take the cable out to the vehicles.

It was an all day job. In the middle of the afternoon I think the snipers were neutralized. That was a big relief.

Before dark we were in firing position and had started to give support to our ground troops who were already advancing inland.

(I found out later I was awarded The Bronze Star for this operation. Never saw it or even read an order until months later.}

Mess Sergeant

JAPANESE PRISONER OF WAR

Prior to the invasion of the Philippines there was a huge demand for intelligence information. The order came to my outfit, "We need POW's.

This was never an easy task or a soft assignment. Taking a Japanese soldier alive was almost impossible since they preferred death rather than being captured. They had been told that Americans unmercifully tortured the Japanese prisoners of war. (In my six years in the service I never heard of one instance of torture by our troops.)

Two days patrolling brought nothing but on the third day we hit it lucky. We had gone deep into a section of the jungle we had not explored before and all of a sudden we hit a bunch of Japs. They were cooking, cutting hair and bathing and we totally surprised them. I guess there were about 40 of them in the camp. We killed them all with the exception of one or two who escaped into the jungle.

We got three Japs alive. We tied them up; stripped their clothing except for loin-cloths and started back to our perimeter (safe area). Two worked themselves loose and started a hassle and we had to shoot them. We made it home with one. It was too late in the day for the pickup by a PT boat. We were shackled with the problem of taking care of this Jap all night long.

At night we were living in "pill boxes" ---a hole about two feet deep and coconut logs (3 or 4) on the sides with firing slits on all four sides.}

None of the guys wanted to keep this Jap overnight in their pill-box so I kept him in mine.

We put him on the floor in the middle of the room, tied his feet to one wall and his hands (behind his back) to the other wall.

We took turns keeping watch over him. My watch was from 3AM to 6AM. I was sitting there in the dark looking at the profile of the man and wondering: Does he have a family? Is he married? Does he have children? There were a million other thoughts running through my mind.

Sometime just before daylight he spoke. I was totally shocked when I heard him say: " I speak a lit-tle English."

I thought I must have drifted off to sleep. I thought---I must be dreaming. But then we began to talk.

To my surprise he said he had spent a year at Harvard.

He was married. He had two children. He said, of course, that he did not want to be in the war; that he did not believe in it; and a lot of other things that you would expect a prisoner of war to say. (I gave him a chocolate bar (D ration) and watched him eat it---giving food to PW's was strictly against the rules.

The next day he was shipped back and I never heard from him again.

But---I always wondered about this man.

Sgt. Thomas

TWO WEEKS R & R (REST AND RELAXATION) IN BRISBANE, AUSTRALIA.

We had been in the line (on the front) for nearly four weeks. We were normally supposed to be relieved every two weeks. I was exhausted. I was tired. I was mad. I was frustrated. I was not thinking clearly and I knew it. I moved like a robot in trying to command the company.

One morning early a message came to me from Division Headquarters. The message read, something like, "Give your company to your second in command and report to General Persons."

I had no idea why I was being called to Division headquarters. I was totally shocked. I followed the messenger back to the rear, got in a jeep and went to Division Headquarters.

I reported to General Persons, saluted and he said:

"Captain DeFoore, our division has been allotted one officer and 60 enlisted men for two weeks R&R in Brisbane Australia. Your name was drawn out of the pot. You are the one officer from the division who gets to go. There is a plane on the strip. Get aboard."

I dropped my grenades and morphine on the ground. I handed my tommy gun to a nearby soldier. I climbed aboard a C-124 transport plane and promptly went to sleep. We flew forever and then someone said; "This is it you guys. All out for Brisbane."

We unloaded. I was taken to a hotel downtown in Brisbane Australia. I met a paymaster who paid me in Dutch guilders. I was given clean uniforms and shoes. I went into the hotel and was assigned a room that I shared with four other officers.

I went to my room. I saw a bed with my name on the pillow. I crawled into the bed with my muddy clothes and boots and slept. I do not know how long.

I finally awakened. I found a shower. I put on a clean uniform. Then to my surprise I was afraid to walk out the door. I went back to my room and sat on my bed. One of the other officers in the room said, "You scared buddy?" I said, "Yes". He said, "Its OK we all were the first day. You will get over it. Go ahead and give it a try."

I went out into the street and started walking-going no-where-just walking. I found a Red Cross food stand and went in and sat down. I ate something. I don't remember what it was. When I tried to pay I found out they did not accept Dutch guilders. Then the Red Cross lady said, "That's OK Yank. Here are some Aussie notes. You can pay me back when you have time."

She thrust a pile of bills into my shirt pocket and said something like she was glad to see me; I must have had a good mother; she knew the war was bad but she hoped I could enjoy Australia. I don't remember the conversation exactly of course but it was something like that.

I was in Australia 19 days. I was supposed to leave after 14 days but could not get a ship going to Morotai for four days. I had five extra days.

I ate 27 steaks and gained 19 pounds in Brisbane.

I met a WAK (Woman's Army Corps) and saw her several times. She was about as goofy as I was so we got along fine. She had been caught in a bombing deal and was pretty traumatized. I don't remember the conversations, but we were comfortable with each other. Never heard from her after I left Brisbane.

I had nightmares every night but the other officers in the room did also. We laughed about this together.

While I was in Brisbane I got the bright idea of buying a refrigerator and taking it back to my outfit. I cabled Telle, my fiancé, and she sent me the money.

I bought the refrigerator and had it crated and took it to the docks to be loaded on a boat going to Morotai. The officer of the deck said that I could not take it because I was only a Captain. I had to be a general to ship a refrigerator.

So I painted out my name and put General Persons name on the box. Immediately it was loaded on the ship.

We made a long trip from Australia to Morotai. Several weeks later we were in the harbor at Morotai to unload. We had an air raid while I had the refrigerator on deck and I was afraid it would get shot up. It did not. However, I painted over General Persons name and put mine there instead. I bribed a truck driver to take the refrigerator to my company area.

From then on---my men had cold beer. We converted a small engine to make the refrigerator work. Guys from adjacent outfits paid a very high price to my men for "cold beer". That refrigerator stayed with my outfit for the remainder of the time in Morotai. I think we lost it on our move to the Philippines.

It was hard for me to get back in the war mood when I returned from Australia. For several days I remember feeling very strange. After a while, my feelings changed and I got back into another frame of mind. I went to my foxhole every night and got up every morning and looked for someone to kill. That was war and I was in the war.

I walked back into hell.

FAMILY IN CAVES

We were advancing slowly up the island of Mindanao. One day as we were moving a scout came to me and said there were people buried in a cave nearby.

We approached the spot with caution. Some of the men started removing branches and dirt from the entrance to the cave on the side of a hill. We made a large opening. There was not a sound from the inside of the cave. I then sent two men with flashlights inside to check the cave and we heard women and children screaming from the inside. They were panicked at the sight of the soldiers. They thought we would kill them like the Japs did.

We finally coaxed them to come out. They were screaming (some of them in English) "Please don't kill us; please don't kill us." We gave them a little of the rations that we could spare.

We finally got the group calmed down and seated under some nearby trees. One of the women came up to me and insisted on knowing, "Who is your wife. I write her a letter and thank her for you-save our life?"

I explained that I had no wife and she said, "OK, OK who is your mama and where can I write to her?" Her insistence finally made me give in and I gave her the name and address of my mother.

(After the war, I saw a copy of the letter that she wrote to my mother thanking her for what we had done to get her family out of the cave.)

There were approximately 35-40 people in the cave. They had fled from a nearby village when the Japs had arrived. They had buried themselves in the cave to escape the Japs.

We shared some of our rations with them and moved on to the next task.

(The rest of the story---I found out from our intelligence crew that after we left the village the Japs had come back the next day and killed every one in the village.)

DEATH OF A FRIEND

These did not make it

We had been in the rest area for nearly two weeks. An order came down for our unit and others to move into the front area.

We were checking ammo, collecting supplies and getting ready for the trip.

Someone said, "Prayer meeting down the line." I went to find the group that was praying." I met with a small group-six or eight-who was standing in a small circle with their arms locked tightly. I got in the group and recognized one of my close friends who was standing by my side.

I nudged him and he nudged back. I noticed that he had on some new jungle boots that had just been issued in the area. I asked where he got them and he said, "New issue. I'll get you a pair when we get back."

We all said a short prayer. Then someone said, "Quickly before we leave everyone give your favorite scripture." I do not remember what anyone said except my friend and I heard him whisper softly:

"Remember now thy Creator in the days of thy youth when the evil days draw nigh..."

We shook hands and left.

Later my unit was moving single file through the jungle to get to the "front". The trail was very narrow and tall grass lined both sides. We had been marching about an hour and the word was passed down: "Stretcher". We immediately moved off the trail into the grass to let the stretcher go by. I looked back as the stretcher passed by. The head and shoulders were covered but then I saw the feet of the person...

and the new boots I had so recently admired. The words ran softly through my mind: "Remember now thy Creator..."

Later I found out that he had moved to the head of his column and out of nowhere a snipers bullet had hit him square in the forehead.

He was a fine man.

He was a clean talker and he lived a clean life.

He had a great smile.

He was brave and gutsy.

He was always a Christian-the kind that made everyone want to be like him.

He was a lieutenant colonel.

SHELL HOLE HUMOR

We were in a firefight. It was the kind where you could not locate the enemy and could not find a place to hide. I was alongside several men and there was a lot of confusion.

There was a sudden burst of machine gun fire and I crawled into a nearby shell hole. I was lying on my back trying to catch my breath when I realized that my new first sergeant was in the same hole with me. His name was Moss.

Moss had a sense of humor. He was always the jokester and took the edge off of serious situations. As we lay there and felt the air rush of the machine gun bullets flying overhead, Moss said: "Long John, those s.o.b.s are using live ammunition. What in the world are they thinking? Don't they know if they keep that up somebody is going to get hurt."

(In the States during training we had practiced crawling through mud while someone was firing blanks at us and it was a sort of a joke.)

We laughed and talked. Then he said, "I think I have had enough of this. I might just go home. I don't think those people out there have nice manners."

We stayed in the hole as long as we could and then decided we had to move. It took a little while but we got out, neutralized the guns. rejoined our troops and moved back into action.

Moments like this kept us sane.

LETTER TO A GRIEVING MOTHER

One of the duties that I had as the commanding officer was to write a letter to the next of kin when a soldier was killed. This was never an easy task but I had to do it more than I wanted to.

We lost a young man one night when we were bombed by the Jap planes. They came just before dawn and dropped two bombs in our company area. All of my men were dug in and their foxholes kept them safe. I do not know why this young man was killed unless he had gotten out of his hole for some reason.

We picked up the body parts and sent them to the rear for burial. The next day I wrote the letter to his mother. It was hard to write, as they all were, but Jack was so young and innocent it seemed a shame that he had to die.

Several months later I got a letter from his mother saying she knew there had been a mistake. She said it was impossible for her son to be dead. She wrote in detail about how much she prayed for him and she knew that God would not allow her son to die.

I was not obligated to respond but I did. I explained with a little detail that he had died and we had buried him.

A month or two later I got another letter from his mother insisting that I explain because she was sure her son was not dead; that he could not be dead because God had promised her that he would bring him home.

I did not respond.

I got no more letters from his mother.

(THE REST OF THE STORY---After the war I received a letter from Jack's sister saying that the mother had never accepted his death. I was asked if I would come to their home and talk with the mother. Reluctantly, I agreed.

I took a plane to their hometown in Michigan and then took a taxi to their address. I met with the family and talked for several hours with the mother and the two sisters. It became obvious to me that she was having a mental breakdown. I knew that there was nothing else I could do so I left.

I got a letter from the sister several weeks later saying that the mother had been committed to a mental hospital.)

DECISION TIME

We had been in the line. I don't know how long. It seemed like for-ever. The whole world seemed like mud, blood and stench. I was try-ing to focus on life, the sun, the sky and breathing to keep my mind clear. Suddenly a messenger appeared and gave me a piece of paper.

I immediately read the instructions and there was a message telling me to report to General Persons at Division Headquarters. My first thought was what have I done? Am I in trouble? But then I did not care because I knew it would be relief for a while and maybe food.

I gave command of the Company to my second, Lt. McKeever, and started to the rear. After walking a while through the jungle I got to the jeep and we bounced over the trail until we arrived at Division Headquarters.

I went to the General's tent, walked in, saluted and reported. General Persons was very kind. He gave me a cup of coffee and a sandwich, which I immediately devoured.

He asked how I was; how things were going; the morale of my men; and other questions. I lied and said things were good.

The General then looked at me and said, "Captain DeFoore, I have a vacancy on my staff and I would like for you to be my Aide de Camp. Give this some thought. Take your time and let me know."

(Aide de Camp is a secretary/assistant to a general officer or high military official.)

I immediately thought, "Oh Boy, good food, sleep on a cot, be in all the meetings, see McArthur" and a lot of other thoughts flooded through my mind.

He then added almost as an afterthought, "Of course you would get a promotion immediately to the rank of Major with a pay raise."

I thought of my men at the front. I went back to the time I had spent training them. I thought of the ones I had buried. Then I knew I could not leave them. I wanted desperately to take the new position but knew in my heart I could not.

I answered immediately. I answered too soon and without proper thought and evaluation. I thanked the General profusely for the offer. I told him I was flattered. Then I said I could not leave my men because they were counting on me.

He was very gracious and kind with my answer and before I left he gave me more food and dry socks and boots.

I felt sad leaving him because I realized he really did want me to be with him.

Six months later General Persons retired. He returned to the States with his entire staff (and I would have been one). He was from a banking family in Montgomery Alabama and I realized over and over that I really had "missed the boat". I would have gone home a year earlier; gotten a immediate raise in pay; and had privileges and opportunities I never dreamed of.

So---I went back to my outfit. One of my officers asked; "What was that all about?" I lied, "No big deal---just administration" crawled in my fox-hole and cried.

I knew I was where I was supposed to be.

EASTER SUNDAY 1944

We had been on a long and difficult patrol. We had hit several pockets of Japs. There were several strong firefights. I was anxious to get back to the secure area, but we kept hitting pockets of resistance.

Finally we broke through and made it home. It was almost dark. We had no food except rations. So there was no call for the evening meal.

It was my responsibility as Commanding Officer to make sure that everyone was dug in every night. I was beyond functioning. I distinctly remember telling my first sergeant Moss to make sure everyone was dug in for the night. I dug a slit trench (a shallow hole so I could lie down vertically and be beneath ground level). I was not sure it was deep enough but I had dug for a few minutes and did not care anymore.

I did not personally make the rounds to make sure everyone was dug in. This was my responsibility as the commanding officer. I failed to do it.

Sometime in the early morning the Japs were making their usual bombing runs. (I was asked if one of my men had started a fire that could be detected by the bombers---I do not think this was true.)

Anyway---we caught 5 bombs in the middle of our company area. I was blown out of my hole and about 10 feet away from my gear. I found my way back in the dark. I began to hear cries of the wounded. I found a medic and we helped several guys that we could find. I turned one man over and in the semidarkness I could see that his chin was gone. I cleaned out his throat and the medic gave him a couple of vials of morphine.

The next morning we counted five dead. Some of the bodies were terribly mangled but we sorted out the body parts as best we could and laced up the panchos to hold the bodies. I commandeered a truck and we hauled the bodies to the temporary cemetery on the beach. There were about ten guys ahead of us waiting to bury and we had to wait an hour to get into the burial area.

It suddenly dawned on me that it was Easter. I have no idea how I knew. I think I felt it rather than thought it. I confirmed this with a chaplain who was passing by. Something deep down on my insides cried and screamed.

I looked at the long line of draped bodies. I looked at the gaunt and sad faces of the men who were bringing the bodies to this place. On my insides I screamed and cried the whole time. Outwardly I did not make a sound. Christ has been raised from the dead. Has he? Where is he? Why did he not stop this insanity? Did He hear my prayer? Was He listening? Did He care? Did He know it was our celebration of his resurrection?

We dug five graves.

We lowered the bodies very carefully.

We listened to the chaplain's prayer.

Some of the guys went swimming in the ocean.

I went back to my outfit, spread my blanket on the ground and went to sleep. Before I closed my eyes—and I have never forgotten this moment---I thanked God for his resurrection.

Worship Service

ESCAPE FROM A TRAP

Somewhere on the island of Morotai I was directed to reconnoiter a certain area to see what the enemy troop concentration was in that area. I do not remember the circumstances but I had eleven men and it was late afternoon.

Our mission was reconnaissance. We were supposed to get information about the enemy position without engaging in a fire-fight.

We finished the task and met no resistance. Late in the afternoon when we were winding our way home we hit an unexpected group of Japs. We were surprised, but they were not. They were waiting for us. It was not long before I realized we were in serious trouble.

We had walked into a trap. We were completely surrounded by Japs and getting fire from every direction. Our situation was absolutely hopeless.

What I am going to say is a mystery. I have never understood how it happened. It just happened.

It is still a mystery to me when I remember this event. But---we had a Marine Air Liaison officer attached to our patrol. (That had never happened before—and it never happened again.)

We were surrounded. We had walked into a trap. I was seriously facing the fact that we might not make it back home.

Then the Marine office crawled up to my side and said, "I have called in a strike and they should be here in a few minutes."

I was stunned. I was so shocked I could not answer. But---in just a few minutes three Vaught Corsair fighters came over with their 50 caliber guns blazing and they were literally plowing the high ground held by the Japanese. Their guns stripped the trees and made the ground look like it had been plowed.

They made three passes, under the direction of the liaison officer. The Japs high tailed it out of the area. Then we were able to move through the lines and start to move back to the safe area.

These planes literally saved my life. I did not ask for air support. I had never had air support before. I had not even thought about the Marine officer being assigned to the patrol. My life as well as the lives of my men were saved by this stranger.

Sometimes I have wondered if that Marine officer was not an angel in disguise.

OUTPOST

I was called to Regimental Headquarters and told to take my company approximately six miles north and up the coast (on Morotai island).

There was a heavy concentration of Japs in that area and we needed protection there.

We loaded into the landing barges and my company was transported to the area. We immediately started building our defensive position. I knew that it would not be long before we were attacked.

We were so far away there would be no artillery support and no phone communication. We did have radio capability sometime.

I had studied defensive positions for a long time and I knew exactly what was required to make my troops safe from attack. We worked for several days to build our defensive position so that we would be reasonably safe.

There was no major attack for two months. After two months

we were told that we would be relieved by another outfit. They were due in the next day.

The new outfit arrived. We loaded in the barges and moved back to the safe area.

Before we left I gave detailed instructions to the new company commander. We had detailed every land mine, booby trap, all the barbed wire and the final lines of fire. We even left two dual mount 50 calibre machine guns we had salvaged from wrecked aircraft.

The second day after we left the Japanese launched a major attack on this position. More than one hundred Imperial Marines (top troops of the Japanese) attacked at midnight. It was a long and bloody night.

We did not lose a single man.

The next day we buried more than one hundred Japanese soldiers in a mass grave outside our perimeter.

It was never defined but I knew that the careful planning I had done for the defense of the position saved the lives of a lot of our troops that night.

HIGH SCHOOL SOLDIER

He came in with a group of replacements. I spotted him immediately. He looked like a child even though he told me he was eighteen years old. I don't think he had even started shaving.

I made sure he did not go on any patrols and gave him a lot of kitchen duty to keep him safe. The other soldiers also seemed to have a protective attitude toward, "Mark".

One night we had a minor attack and a few Japs were killed trying to infiltrate our area. I learned that Mark had killed a Jap during the attack.

We had a rule that whenever you killed a Jap in our area you had the responsibility of disposing of the body. You had to bury it.

I was walking through the area and I found Mark digging the hole to bury the Jap. I called his attention to the fact that the hole was too short and not long enough to bury the body.

Mark answered, "Yes I know that. I am going to chop off his legs and throw them in."

I looked at him. He showed no feelings. He did not apologize for the statement. Apparently he felt nothing. He turned around and kept digging.

I walked away stunned. Later I heard him laughing with a group who helped him with the body.

LOSS OF ONE MAN

We ran into a hornet's nest.

The patrol had been rather quiet until we found ourselves in the midst of another Jap patrol who had entered the same area we were searching.

We fanned out in firing positions to protect ourselves. We set up a good fire-base but it soon became obvious that the Japs were bringing in reinforcements.

We had none. I had, I think, nine men. We continued to fire and inflicted quite a few casualties on the Japs. (On the whole I think the American soldiers were better shots than the Japs-except for their snipers. They were deadly.)

I realized very soon that we were overpowered and began looking for an escape route to get the patrol back home.

We started pulling back very slowly while holding a strong line of front fire. As I was crawling to the front I found one of my men had been hit in the spine and both of his legs were paralyzed.

Our eyes met just for a moment. In that moment I knew it was over for him---he knew that it was over for him---we both knew that it was over.

We were overpowered and outgunned.

We had to retreat to save the remaining troops.

There was no stretcher—no medics.

We could have stayed and all died.

or—we could leave this guy and save the rest

so---I made the decision to leave the wounded man.

When I got back to where I had left him I started to tell him the situation but he stopped me. He said, "Hey man, don't say it. I know the drill. Give me all your grenades and some more morphine and get your tail out of here. I will be OK and I will get a few more of those s.o.b.s before they get me."

Then this crazy guy started singing a popular tune, "Don't get around much anymore."

I reached out to shake his hand. He refused. I left,

The next day I came back with a reinforced patrol to pick up the body. It was not there.

I have never forgotten the moment---or the man.

I have never forgotten the words to the song.

VISIT TO NATIVE VILLAGE

On Morotai and Mindanao in the Philippines there were times when we had a Red Cross person assigned to our outfit.

When we were in rest camp this person, the Regimental surgeon (Major Burgess) and I would go to a nearby native village.

The main purpose was to give medical help, which was provided by Major Burgess the medical officer. I collected as many T-shirts, socks, shoes and any other discarded items of clothing as I could. The Red Cross guy had packets of toothpaste, toothbrushes, band-aids and skin ointment that he could give to the people.

Our arrival at the village was a big, big, moment. The people in the village all lined up to "See the Doctor". Some had no ailments---these got a band aid on their hand or arm where they could show it to their friends. Some were seriously ill. There were a few cases of leprosy; lots of complications due to malaria. There were always open sores that needed treatment. All the children had distended bellies, which I think (though I am not sure) was caused by an enlarged spleen and malaria.

The Red Cross man and I distributed our "stuff' as the doctor saw the people in line. They were all very grateful for anything we gave them. They would sing and dance when we gave them the least and smallest gift. Their gratitude was dramatic and moving. The natives were very proud of their bandages. The band aids were worn like a badge of courage.

Each time, when we were leaving a village the people would line our path—their hand cupped, prayer like, before their face---and they bowed and sang to us as we were leaving. I could hardly hold back my tears.

(This was in stark contrast to the way the Japs treated them. They usually raped the women and young girls and used the men as servants.)

This was a welcome relief from the war. It introduced an element of sanity into the insanity of the war.

Work Crew

FOX HOLES, SLIT TRENCHES AND PILL BOXES

The Japs were persistent night fighters. They searched for American positions or instillations and attacked at night. One jap soldier could threaten a group at night with random rifle fire or a few grenades. It was necessary, it was imperative, that the troops were protected at night

The main protection was the fox hole. (I think the term originated with the Germans in WWI.) This was a hole in the ground big enough for one, and rarely two, soldiers. It was best when seats were dug out so that the soldier could sit and not just slump in the hole. Late afternoons were usually spent preparing for the night. You need water at night. You must have taken care of your toilet needs before dark. There was no getting out of the hole at night.

The fresh dirt had to be removed from the area of the hole so it would not be obvious. Or the dirt could be camouflaged with grass or branches. Whenever there was time, or the ground was soft some soldiers dug pockets in the dirt walls for cigarettes or socks or shoes.

When dark came, every person had to be in a hole. You shot in the direction of every movement at night. No one ever got out of a hole and moved around after dark. Every movement at night was considered to be an enemy.

The other protection at night was called a "Slit trench". Whenever there was not enough time or whenever there was too much coral, soldiers would dig a shallow trench, and hopefully get their body below the surface of the ground. (The person would lie down in the trench.) This of course did not provide as much protection but at times it was all that could be done. A soldier in a slit trench was much more vulnerable than one in a fox hole. Slit trenches provided little or no protection from air raids.

In stable situations when troops planned to be in a position for an extended period "Pill boxes" were constructed. A hole was dug two or three feet in the ground (this was determined by the hardness of the soil-or the presence of coral). The hole was usually ten feet square. Then three or four coconut logs were stacked on each side. Firing slits were cut on each side for defense at night. The top was covered with coconut logs also.

Usually four persons slept in a pill box. If cots were available that was a luxury, or beds could be made out of coconut or palm branches.

Inside the pill box the ceiling height was usually about four feet. It was a little awkward to move around on the inside. Occasionally there were snakes but this was not considered a big problem

DELIRIUM

This is the hardest part for me to write. I had rather not write it but it is a necessary part of the story.

I am not sure about the accuracy of the details. In my thinking it is mostly a blur.

But I remember a few events very well.

I had left my original company because I had been promoted from Captain to Major. I think this was a mistake. I should have stayed with my old outfit. I went to the Second Battalion as Battalion Executive. In hindsight, I should have refused the promotion.

Later I was sent on a special mission to meet up with a group of Philippine volunteers from Davao City. I think this was near the East Coast of Mindanao. I was to lead them back to our outfit.

I left my outfit with two other guys. We had three days rations.

We left at night because we had to go through the Japanese held area. The first night we ran into the trouble. There was a brief firefight. The next morning there were two of us. I never knew what happened to the other guy. We travelled east as much as I could using my compass.

I do not think we ever made it through the Jap held area. The next few days were very bad. The Japanese soldiers were every way I turned. Sometime in the next few days I lost the other guy. I think he stepped on a booby trap.

I kept trying to move to the East with little or no success. Of course I could only travel at night. In the daytime I had to bury myself with brush or find a hole. I was completely surrounded by Japs. For a while I slept most of the day.

I had no food. I looked for anything I could eat. I ate bananas (sometimes green), pineapples, coconut milk, papayas, mangos, roots (similar to potatoes), and the leaves of some plants that I knew were safe to eat. My movement in the day was very limited of course so I scavenged for food at night.

I had very little water. My tongue had swollen and I had trouble closing my mouth. For the first few days I picked the leaches off my body at night. Finally I stopped doing this. I had dysentery very bad.

I remember one moment distinctly. I had buried myself in an embankment near a road before the sun came up. I always made my cover so I could see outside. Sometime during the day a

Japanese soldier came and sat down about ten yards from where I was buried. He took a drink of water from his canteen and lit a cigarette.

I desperately wanted the water and the cigarette even though I had stopped smoking months earlier.

I thought about shooting him but I knew that would be the end of me. I thought about running and cutting his throat with my knife. I wanted the water and the cigarette desperately.

I decided, gratefully, to do nothing. That probably saved my life.

I think this lasted two or three weeks. I lost all track of time. I tried to find my way back to my outfit. Other times I just tried to find water and something to eat. There were times when I halluci-nated when I was buried during the day. I wandered like an animal, not knowing or caring where I was going.

I was just trying to stay alive. I was in the middle of the Jap held area and could not find a way out.

One night I knew that I was dying. I thought that I would die and my body would not be found. I wanted desperately for someone to find me. Sometime in the night I heard vehicles moving. I started moving in the direction of the sounds.

I distinctly remember finding a road. I lay down across the road so someone---the Japs or my troops---would find me---and lost consciousness.

The next thing I knew---a woman, a nurse, was calling my name and telling me to wake up.

I was on a cot. I was in a tent. I did not know if it was a Jap or American. I was terrified and my first thought was escape.

I could not rise. I could not sit up

The nurse (American) was trying to put a spoon of soup in my mouth. I do remember that I fought her. I remember too that she laughed and smiled.

I was terrified. I was absolutely panicked. I was totally and completely crazy.

Some time later I could think more clearly. There was a man on the cot next to me. In the night I think he died. I saw two men come and put his body on a stretcher. Then I decided I was in a Jap hospital. I tried to stand up so I could leave and my IV suddenly told me I could not. The nurse came and talked to me. She was wearing perfume.

I listened to her. I got back on my cot.

I was transferred to another hospital. All the leeches and ticks were gone. My tongue returned to normal and I felt better. It was several days, I guess, before I realized I was safe and in an American hospital.

My body could not accept food. I vomited all day and my diarrhea seemed to get worse. I felt every day that I was going to die. I just wanted to die so the agony would be over. The nausea was unbelievable. At one point I remember that I stopped eating.

The details of what happened to me at this time are very vague. I do remember that I felt every day that I was going to die. I also remember that I desperately wanted to die but there was always the thought in my mind, "Do not die. Do not die. Do not die."

After two months, as well as I can remember I think I was transferred to another hospital. One day I realized I was being loaded onto a ship. I wanted desperately to escape. I did not want to be put on a hospital ship but I could not stand; I could not run; I was still lost.

HOSPITAL SHIP

The hospital ship was heaven. Some time after I boarded I began to digest my food and the dysentery stopped. I was transferred to another ward on the ship and given some clothes. I started to think better and realized that I was going to live. I realized that I was going home.

I felt guilty for leaving my outfit. I felt guilty for leaving my men. I felt guilty for being sick. I had a horrible time for a while. One day a chaplain came and talked to me for a long time. I stated to feel much better.

The journey home took forty-five days. I met a German doctor who taught me to play chess. I started to walk again. However my thinking was not good. I was suicidal at times. I thought about jumping overboard. I thought about cutting my wrists. I thought about other ways of ending my life.

One day I was talking with the Chaplain. I heard him say, "Hell, Man, you fought to stay alive all this time. Why in the world are you trying to end the life you worked so hard to save?"

Suddenly he made sense. The suicide drive was greatly diminished and I began to think more clearly. I started to think about home, my family, my fiancé and my home town.

My sanity began to return. I know you will find this hard to understand but sanity seemed very strange to me.

THE END

I landed in New York the day it was announced that we had dropped an atomic bomb on Hiroshima---August 6, 1945.

We were transported from the ship to Halloran General Hospital.

That night everyone was celebrating the fact that the war was ended. I borrowed a uniform from a navy attendant. I caught a bus to Times Square in New York.

Suddenly I found myself in front of a War Surplus Store. It was closed. I banged on the door until someone came. I explained to the man that I had no money but needed a uniform. He gave me a complete dress uniform and told me to send him the money when I got home. (I did.)

I went back to Times Square. Everyone was screaming and shouting and laughing and I was terrified. I stayed close to a building for a while and then I got a bus and went back to the hospital.

Later I was transferred to a hospital In Camp Butner North Carolina. I spent four months in this hospital and was discharged from the service on January 6, 1946.

HOME

Sometime in the closing days of August I came home. I had a month leave of absence from the hospital.

I had no vehicle of course so my only means of travel was on the Greyhound bus. I boarded in the early morning for the 750 mile trip.

The bus was filled with soldiers. I talked with no one. I was very frightened. I was not sure I could make the trip. I seriously considered getting off the bus and going back to the hospital but very quickly we pulled out and I was on my way to Mississippi.

Thoughts flooded my mind like an overflowing river. I immediately had pictures of home, my mother, my fiance Telle, the Church, the river and the river-bank.

Most of all I pictured my three brothers. Two of them, Grady and Charles, were already home—Grady from the Marines and Charles from the Sea-Bees. We were waiting for news from Jud, my youngest brother on a sub in the Mediterranean.

The bus ride was long. We made frequent stops. I slept. I cried. I fantasied about seeing everyone. I planned to act "normal" but did not know if I could. I thought about turning around and going back to the hospital.

I felt more comfortable with the thought of being in the hospital than I felt about being at home with my family.

I went back to sleep.

Finally---

I was in Greenwood, Mississippi at the bus station.

My brother Grady was there to pick me up and we made the seven-mile trip to Sidon. We talked very little. We laughed some. He was reassuring.

We pulled up in front of the house. It was the same.

I got out of the car and walked into the arms of my Mother and Charles.

Two weeks later I married Tetelle Topp in Moorhead, Mississippi.

THE END---BUT NOT THE END

The war never ended for me.

I have carried it in my heart, my head, my soul, my spirit---somewhere every day and every night that I have lived.

I pray every day to forget what I did not want to remember.

Memories lie there dormant in my heart and wait for me to lie down at night and go to sleep. It hides in the back of my mind all day.

And at night, the memories pour out of the past.

The Japs storm into my bedroom. The bombers scream overhead. The wounded cry and scream in pain asking for help. The staccato roar of the machine gun burns my brain.

I am catapulted out of bed-screaming, cursing, swearing and crying trying to make sense out of the senseless situation that is taking place in my head. It is more real than my breath. I can visibly see the scenes. I can hear the whine of the bombs and the blast of air that comes when they explode. The machine gun blast takes my breath. The cries of the wounded seem to tear across the fabric of my heart and my sleep. I try to find what I am supposed to do in the battle.

Then my wife---Thank God---keeps calling my name and saying. "It is all right. Honey, everything is OK. You are home. I am here. Please stop. OK. Everything is all right. Drink some water. Look at me. Wake up. Everything is OK . I am here. I am here. Don't hit. Don't hit me."---until I can finally hear her and see her and realize where I am, and realize who I am.

Sometimes I cry in relief. I am embarrassed. Often I feel shame. I am so surprised to find myself in reality. I am in my home and there is no war.

I wait for the daylight. I wait for the sunrise. I wait for sanity. When daylight comes I am always relieved. The darkness is such a threat and a demon.

This does not happen every night. Sometimes I have a week with no trauma. Other times it comes more often. I cannot find the triggers. It just seems to happen.

They call it PTSD—post traumatic stress syndrome.

I have another word for it—hell.

I guess for me the war will never end---

until the bugler blows taps for me—

and the guns fire the salute---

then they will fold the flag---

lay it gently into the hands of Marion Sue--

and I shall rest---

and the war will have ended--

and God will give me peace in my heart.

FINIS

POST SCRIPT

There are some stories I cannot write. This is not the whole story. I remember events sometimes and tell myself it is not true. I tell myself it never happened.

War is insanity and when humans are insane all reason, logic, integrity and humanity vanish.

I have seen things, that when I recall them, I do not believe myself. Yet I cannot forget or deny them.

Neither will I confess and claim them.

God knows the whole story.

He has assured me of forgiveness.

CPSIA information can be obtained
at www.ICGtesting.com
Printed in the USA
BVHW030534181118
533265BV00002B/6/P